50 Cheese-Lover's Dishes

By: Kelly Johnson

Table of Contents

- Macaroni and Cheese
- Four Cheese Pizza
- Cheese Fondue
- Grilled Cheese Sandwich
- Cheese Ravioli
- Cheese Quesadilla
- Cheddar Biscuits
- Mozzarella Sticks
- Cheese Croquettes
- Brie and Fig Tart
- Caprese Salad
- Cheese Soufflé
- Baked Ziti with Ricotta
- Cheddar and Chive Scones
- Baked Mac and Cheese Casserole
- Cheese Frittata
- Cheese and Spinach Stuffed Mushrooms
- Cheese Enchiladas
- Cheese and Ham Croissant
- Goat Cheese Salad
- Baked Brie with Honey and Almonds
- Blue Cheese Dressing
- Grilled Cheese and Tomato Soup
- Cheese and Garlic Bread
- Cheesy Potato Gratin
- Cheese Tortellini
- Cheeseburger
- Pizza Margherita
- Raclette with Potatoes and Charcuterie
- Cottage Cheese Pancakes
- Cheese Nachos
- Cheese Puffs
- Mac and Cheese Pizza
- Baked Cheese-Stuffed Peppers
- Cheese Focaccia

- Cheese and Herb Crackers
- Fondue-stuffed Chicken
- Cheese-stuffed Meatballs
- Burrata with Roasted Vegetables
- Roquefort Salad with Pears
- Cheese and Spinach Calzone
- Halloumi Fries
- Sweet and Savory Cheese Strudels
- Eggplant Parmesan
- Ricotta Cheesecake
- Cheddar Popcorn
- Goat Cheese and Beet Salad
- Cheese-Stuffed Puffs
- Grilled Cheese with Pesto
- Smoked Gouda Mac and Cheese

Macaroni and Cheese

Ingredients:

- 8 oz elbow macaroni
- 2 cups shredded sharp cheddar cheese
- 1 cup milk
- 1/2 cup heavy cream
- 3 tablespoons butter
- 3 tablespoons all-purpose flour
- 1/4 teaspoon salt
- 1/4 teaspoon black pepper
- 1/4 teaspoon paprika (optional)
- 1/4 teaspoon garlic powder (optional)

Instructions:

1. Cook the elbow macaroni according to package instructions. Drain and set aside.
2. In a large saucepan, melt butter over medium heat. Stir in the flour and cook for 1-2 minutes.
3. Gradually whisk in the milk and heavy cream, and cook until the sauce thickens.
4. Stir in the shredded cheddar cheese and season with salt, pepper, paprika, and garlic powder.
5. Combine the cooked macaroni with the cheese sauce and stir until well-coated.
6. Serve warm.

Four Cheese Pizza

Ingredients:

- 1 pizza dough (store-bought or homemade)
- 1/2 cup tomato sauce
- 1 cup shredded mozzarella cheese
- 1/2 cup crumbled blue cheese
- 1/2 cup grated Parmesan cheese
- 1/2 cup shredded provolone cheese
- Fresh basil leaves (optional)

Instructions:

1. Preheat the oven to 475°F (245°C).
2. Roll out the pizza dough on a floured surface to your desired size.
3. Spread the tomato sauce evenly over the dough.
4. Sprinkle the mozzarella, blue cheese, Parmesan, and provolone over the sauce.
5. Bake the pizza in the preheated oven for 10-12 minutes, or until the cheese is melted and bubbly.
6. Garnish with fresh basil leaves (optional) and serve hot.

Cheese Fondue

Ingredients:

- 1 cup shredded Gruyère cheese
- 1 cup shredded Emmental cheese
- 1 tablespoon lemon juice
- 1 clove garlic, halved
- 1 cup dry white wine
- 1 tablespoon cornstarch
- 1 tablespoon kirsch (cherry brandy, optional)
- Freshly ground black pepper, to taste
- Freshly grated nutmeg, to taste
- Cubed bread, vegetables, or fruits for dipping

Instructions:

1. Rub the inside of a fondue pot with the cut sides of the garlic.
2. In a separate pot, heat the wine and lemon juice over medium heat until hot, but not boiling.
3. Gradually add the shredded cheese, stirring constantly until melted.
4. Mix the cornstarch with kirsch (if using), then add to the cheese mixture to thicken.
5. Season with black pepper and nutmeg.
6. Serve the cheese fondue with cubed bread, vegetables, or fruits for dipping.

Grilled Cheese Sandwich

Ingredients:

- 2 slices of bread
- 2 slices of cheddar cheese
- 1 tablespoon butter

Instructions:

1. Butter one side of each slice of bread.
2. Place a slice of cheese between the two slices of bread, buttered side facing out.
3. Heat a skillet over medium heat and place the sandwich in the skillet.
4. Grill until golden brown on both sides, about 3-4 minutes per side.
5. Serve hot.

Cheese Ravioli

Ingredients:

- 12 oz cheese ravioli (store-bought or homemade)
- 1/4 cup olive oil
- 1 clove garlic, minced
- 1/4 teaspoon red pepper flakes (optional)
- Fresh basil leaves, chopped
- 1/4 cup grated Parmesan cheese
- Salt and pepper to taste

Instructions:

1. Cook the ravioli according to package instructions.
2. While the ravioli cooks, heat olive oil in a skillet over medium heat. Add the garlic and red pepper flakes, sautéing for 1-2 minutes.
3. Once the ravioli is cooked, drain and add to the skillet. Toss to coat in the garlic oil.
4. Season with salt and pepper, and garnish with fresh basil and grated Parmesan.
5. Serve hot.

Cheese Quesadilla

Ingredients:

- 2 flour tortillas
- 1 cup shredded cheddar cheese
- 1/2 cup shredded mozzarella cheese
- 1/4 cup sliced jalapeños (optional)
- Butter for cooking

Instructions:

1. Heat a skillet over medium heat and add a little butter.
2. Place one tortilla in the skillet and sprinkle with a mixture of cheddar and mozzarella cheeses.
3. If desired, add sliced jalapeños for a spicy kick.
4. Place the second tortilla on top and cook for 2-3 minutes on each side, until golden brown and the cheese is melted.
5. Slice and serve with salsa or guacamole.

Cheddar Biscuits

Ingredients:

- 2 cups all-purpose flour
- 1 tablespoon baking powder
- 1/2 teaspoon salt
- 1/2 teaspoon garlic powder (optional)
- 1/2 cup cold butter, cubed
- 1 cup shredded cheddar cheese
- 3/4 cup milk

Instructions:

1. Preheat the oven to 450°F (230°C).
2. In a large bowl, combine the flour, baking powder, salt, and garlic powder.
3. Cut in the cold butter until the mixture resembles coarse crumbs.
4. Stir in the shredded cheddar cheese and milk until just combined.
5. Drop spoonfuls of dough onto a greased baking sheet.
6. Bake for 10-12 minutes, or until golden brown.
7. Serve warm.

Mozzarella Sticks

Ingredients:

- 8 oz mozzarella cheese, cut into sticks
- 1 cup all-purpose flour
- 2 large eggs, beaten
- 1 cup breadcrumbs
- 1/2 teaspoon garlic powder
- 1/2 teaspoon dried oregano
- Vegetable oil, for frying

Instructions:

1. Coat the mozzarella sticks in flour, then dip in the beaten eggs, and finally coat with breadcrumbs mixed with garlic powder and oregano.
2. Heat vegetable oil in a skillet or deep fryer over medium heat.
3. Fry the mozzarella sticks for 2-3 minutes, or until golden and crispy.
4. Drain on paper towels and serve with marinara sauce.

Cheese Croquettes

Ingredients:

- 1 cup mashed potatoes
- 1/2 cup grated cheddar cheese
- 1/4 cup breadcrumbs
- 1/4 teaspoon garlic powder
- 1 egg, beaten
- Vegetable oil, for frying

Instructions:

1. In a bowl, combine mashed potatoes, cheddar cheese, breadcrumbs, and garlic powder. Mix well.
2. Shape the mixture into small balls or oval shapes.
3. Dip each croquette into the beaten egg and coat with breadcrumbs.
4. Heat vegetable oil in a skillet over medium heat.
5. Fry the croquettes for 3-4 minutes, or until golden brown and crispy.
6. Drain on paper towels and serve hot.

Brie and Fig Tart

Ingredients:

- 1 sheet puff pastry
- 8 oz Brie cheese, sliced
- 1/2 cup fig jam
- 1/4 cup fresh thyme leaves
- Salt and pepper to taste
- 1 egg (for egg wash)

Instructions:

1. Preheat the oven to 375°F (190°C).
2. Roll out the puff pastry onto a baking sheet lined with parchment paper.
3. Spread a thin layer of fig jam over the pastry, leaving a small border around the edges.
4. Arrange slices of Brie cheese on top of the fig jam.
5. Sprinkle with fresh thyme leaves, and season with salt and pepper.
6. Fold the edges of the puff pastry over the filling to create a rustic tart shape.
7. Brush the edges of the pastry with the beaten egg.
8. Bake for 20-25 minutes, or until the pastry is golden brown and the cheese is melted.
9. Serve warm.

Caprese Salad

Ingredients:

- 2 large tomatoes, sliced
- 8 oz fresh mozzarella cheese, sliced
- Fresh basil leaves
- Olive oil
- Balsamic vinegar
- Salt and pepper to taste

Instructions:

1. Arrange the tomato and mozzarella slices alternately on a serving platter.
2. Tuck fresh basil leaves between the tomato and cheese slices.
3. Drizzle with olive oil and balsamic vinegar.
4. Season with salt and pepper to taste.
5. Serve immediately as a refreshing appetizer or side dish.

Cheese Soufflé

Ingredients:

- 3 tablespoons butter
- 3 tablespoons all-purpose flour
- 1 cup milk
- 1 cup shredded Gruyère or cheddar cheese
- 1/4 teaspoon salt
- 1/4 teaspoon ground white pepper
- 1/4 teaspoon mustard powder (optional)
- 4 large eggs, separated
- 1/4 teaspoon cream of tartar

Instructions:

1. Preheat the oven to 375°F (190°C) and butter a soufflé dish.
2. In a saucepan, melt the butter over medium heat. Stir in the flour and cook for 1-2 minutes.
3. Gradually add the milk, whisking constantly, until the mixture thickens and is smooth.
4. Remove from heat and stir in the shredded cheese, salt, pepper, and mustard powder.
5. Beat the egg yolks in a bowl and stir them into the cheese mixture.
6. In a separate bowl, beat the egg whites with cream of tartar until stiff peaks form.
7. Gently fold the egg whites into the cheese mixture.
8. Pour the mixture into the prepared soufflé dish.
9. Bake for 25-30 minutes, or until the soufflé has risen and is golden brown.
10. Serve immediately.

Baked Ziti with Ricotta

Ingredients:

- 1 lb ziti pasta
- 2 cups ricotta cheese
- 2 cups marinara sauce
- 2 cups shredded mozzarella cheese
- 1/2 cup grated Parmesan cheese
- 1/4 cup chopped fresh basil
- Salt and pepper to taste

Instructions:

1. Preheat the oven to 375°F (190°C).
2. Cook the ziti pasta according to package instructions. Drain and set aside.
3. In a large bowl, mix the ricotta cheese, 1 cup of mozzarella, Parmesan, and fresh basil. Season with salt and pepper.
4. In a baking dish, spread a thin layer of marinara sauce on the bottom.
5. Layer the cooked ziti on top of the sauce, then spoon the ricotta mixture over the pasta.
6. Pour the remaining marinara sauce over the ricotta mixture and sprinkle the remaining mozzarella cheese on top.
7. Bake for 20-25 minutes, or until the cheese is melted and bubbly.
8. Serve warm.

Cheddar and Chive Scones

Ingredients:

- 2 cups all-purpose flour
- 1 tablespoon baking powder
- 1/2 teaspoon salt
- 1/2 cup cold butter, cubed
- 1 cup shredded cheddar cheese
- 1/4 cup chopped fresh chives
- 1/2 cup buttermilk
- 1 egg (for egg wash)

Instructions:

1. Preheat the oven to 400°F (200°C) and line a baking sheet with parchment paper.
2. In a large bowl, combine flour, baking powder, and salt.
3. Cut in the cold butter until the mixture resembles coarse crumbs.
4. Stir in the shredded cheddar cheese and chopped chives.
5. Add the buttermilk and mix until the dough just comes together.
6. Turn the dough onto a floured surface and knead gently. Pat the dough into a 1-inch thick round and cut into wedges.
7. Place the wedges on the baking sheet and brush with a beaten egg.
8. Bake for 15-20 minutes, or until golden brown.
9. Serve warm.

Baked Mac and Cheese Casserole

Ingredients:

- 1 lb elbow macaroni
- 4 tablespoons butter
- 4 tablespoons all-purpose flour
- 4 cups milk
- 2 cups shredded sharp cheddar cheese
- 1 cup shredded mozzarella cheese
- 1/2 teaspoon salt
- 1/2 teaspoon black pepper
- 1/4 teaspoon garlic powder
- 1/2 cup breadcrumbs

Instructions:

1. Preheat the oven to 350°F (175°C).
2. Cook the elbow macaroni according to package instructions. Drain and set aside.
3. In a saucepan, melt butter over medium heat. Stir in the flour and cook for 1-2 minutes.
4. Gradually whisk in the milk and cook until the sauce thickens.
5. Stir in the cheddar cheese, mozzarella cheese, salt, pepper, and garlic powder until the cheese is melted.
6. Combine the cooked macaroni with the cheese sauce and stir to coat.
7. Pour the mixture into a greased baking dish. Top with breadcrumbs.
8. Bake for 25-30 minutes, or until the top is golden and bubbly.
9. Serve warm.

Cheese Frittata

Ingredients:

- 8 large eggs
- 1/2 cup milk
- 1 cup shredded cheese (such as cheddar, mozzarella, or feta)
- 1/4 cup chopped fresh spinach
- 1/4 cup chopped onions
- Salt and pepper to taste
- 1 tablespoon olive oil

Instructions:

1. Preheat the oven to 375°F (190°C).
2. In a bowl, whisk the eggs with milk, salt, and pepper.
3. Stir in the shredded cheese and chopped spinach.
4. Heat the olive oil in an oven-safe skillet over medium heat. Add the onions and sauté until softened, about 3 minutes.
5. Pour the egg mixture into the skillet and cook for 3-4 minutes, without stirring.
6. Transfer the skillet to the oven and bake for 10-15 minutes, or until the eggs are set and golden.
7. Serve warm.

Cheese and Spinach Stuffed Mushrooms

Ingredients:

- 12 large mushroom caps, stems removed
- 1 cup ricotta cheese
- 1/2 cup shredded mozzarella cheese
- 1/4 cup grated Parmesan cheese
- 1/2 cup cooked spinach, squeezed dry
- 1 garlic clove, minced
- 1 tablespoon olive oil
- Salt and pepper to taste

Instructions:

1. Preheat the oven to 375°F (190°C).
2. In a bowl, combine ricotta cheese, mozzarella cheese, Parmesan, cooked spinach, garlic, salt, and pepper.
3. Spoon the cheese mixture into the mushroom caps.
4. Place the stuffed mushrooms on a baking sheet and drizzle with olive oil.
5. Bake for 15-20 minutes, or until the mushrooms are tender and the cheese is melted.
6. Serve warm.

Cheese Enchiladas

Ingredients:

- 10 corn tortillas
- 2 cups shredded cheddar cheese
- 1/2 cup chopped onion
- 1/2 cup sour cream
- 1 cup enchilada sauce
- 1/4 teaspoon cumin
- 1/4 teaspoon chili powder
- Salt and pepper to taste

Instructions:

1. Preheat the oven to 350°F (175°C).
2. Warm the corn tortillas in a dry skillet or microwave.
3. In a bowl, combine the shredded cheddar cheese, chopped onion, cumin, chili powder, salt, and pepper.
4. Spoon the cheese mixture into each tortilla and roll them up tightly.
5. Place the rolled tortillas in a baking dish, seam-side down.
6. Pour the enchilada sauce over the top of the rolled tortillas and sprinkle with extra cheese.
7. Bake for 20-25 minutes, or until the cheese is melted and bubbly.
8. Serve with sour cream.

Cheese and Ham Croissant

Ingredients:

- 4 croissants
- 8 oz ham, thinly sliced
- 8 oz Swiss cheese, sliced
- 2 tablespoons Dijon mustard (optional)
- 1 egg (for egg wash)

Instructions:

1. Preheat the oven to 375°F (190°C).
2. Slice the croissants in half horizontally, but not all the way through.
3. Spread Dijon mustard on the bottom half of each croissant (optional).
4. Layer the ham and Swiss cheese inside the croissant.
5. Place the croissants on a baking sheet and brush the tops with a beaten egg for a golden finish.
6. Bake for 10-12 minutes, or until the cheese is melted and the croissants are golden brown.
7. Serve warm.

Goat Cheese Salad

Ingredients:

- 4 cups mixed greens (arugula, spinach, or lettuce)
- 4 oz goat cheese, crumbled
- 1/2 cup walnuts, toasted
- 1/4 cup dried cranberries
- 1/4 red onion, thinly sliced
- 1 tablespoon balsamic vinegar
- 2 tablespoons olive oil
- Salt and pepper to taste

Instructions:

1. In a large bowl, combine the mixed greens, crumbled goat cheese, toasted walnuts, dried cranberries, and sliced red onion.
2. In a small bowl, whisk together the balsamic vinegar, olive oil, salt, and pepper.
3. Drizzle the dressing over the salad and toss to combine.
4. Serve immediately.

Baked Brie with Honey and Almonds

Ingredients:

- 1 wheel of Brie cheese
- 1/4 cup sliced almonds
- 2 tablespoons honey
- Fresh thyme (optional)

Instructions:

1. Preheat the oven to 350°F (175°C).
2. Place the Brie wheel on a baking sheet lined with parchment paper.
3. Sprinkle the sliced almonds over the top of the Brie.
4. Drizzle honey over the almonds and cheese.
5. Bake for 10-12 minutes, or until the cheese is soft and slightly melted.
6. Garnish with fresh thyme if desired and serve with crackers or bread.

Blue Cheese Dressing

Ingredients:

- 1/2 cup mayonnaise
- 1/2 cup sour cream
- 1/4 cup buttermilk
- 1/4 cup crumbled blue cheese
- 1 tablespoon lemon juice
- Salt and pepper to taste

Instructions:

1. In a bowl, whisk together the mayonnaise, sour cream, and buttermilk.
2. Stir in the crumbled blue cheese and lemon juice.
3. Season with salt and pepper to taste.
4. Chill in the fridge for 30 m nutes before serving. Enjoy with salads or as a dip.

Grilled Cheese and Tomato Soup

Ingredients for Grilled Cheese:

- 8 slices bread (white, whole wheat, or sourdough)
- 4 tablespoons butter
- 8 oz cheddar cheese, sliced or shredded

Ingredients for Tomato Soup:

- 1 can (14 oz) diced tomatoes
- 1 cup vegetable broth
- 1/2 cup heavy cream
- 1 tablespoon olive oil
- 1 small onion, chopped
- 1 garlic clove, minced
- Salt and pepper to taste
- Fresh basil (optional)

Instructions for Grilled Cheese:

1. Butter one side of each slice of bread.
2. Place a slice of cheese between two slices of bread, buttered sides facing out.
3. Heat a skillet over medium heat and grill the sandwich on both sides until golden brown and the cheese is melted.
4. Serve warm.

Instructions for Tomato Soup:

1. Heat olive oil in a saucepan over medium heat.
2. Add chopped onion and garlic, and cook until softened, about 3 minutes.
3. Add diced tomatoes and vegetable broth. Simmer for 15-20 minutes.
4. Stir in the heavy cream and season with salt and pepper.
5. Puree the soup with an immersion blender or in a regular blender until smooth.
6. Garnish with fresh basil and serve alongside grilled cheese.

Cheese and Garlic Bread

Ingredients:

- 1 loaf French baguette or Italian bread
- 4 tablespoons butter, softened
- 3 garlic cloves, minced
- 1 cup shredded mozzarella cheese
- 1/2 cup grated Parmesan cheese
- 1 tablespoon fresh parsley, chopped

Instructions:

1. Preheat the oven to 375°F (190°C).
2. Slice the loaf of bread in half lengthwise.
3. Mix the softened butter with minced garlic, mozzarella cheese, Parmesan, and parsley.
4. Spread the garlic butter mixture evenly over the cut sides of the bread.
5. Place the bread on a baking sheet and bake for 10-12 minutes, until the cheese is melted and golden brown.
6. Slice and serve warm.

Cheesy Potato Gratin

Ingredients:

- 4 large russet potatoes, thinly sliced
- 2 cups heavy cream
- 1 cup shredded Gruyère cheese
- 1/2 cup grated Parmesan cheese
- 2 cloves garlic, minced
- 2 tablespoons butter
- Salt and pepper to taste

Instructions:

1. Preheat the oven to 375°F (190°C).
2. Butter a baking dish and layer the sliced potatoes, overlapping each layer slightly.
3. In a saucepan, heat the heavy cream and garlic over medium heat until warm.
4. Pour the cream over the potatoes and sprinkle with Gruyère, Parmesan, salt, and pepper.
5. Dot the top with butter and cover with foil.
6. Bake for 45 minutes, then remove the foil and bake for an additional 20 minutes, until the top is golden and the potatoes are tender.
7. Serve warm.

Cheese Tortellini

Ingredients:

- 1 package cheese tortellini (fresh or frozen)
- 2 cups marinara sauce or Alfredo sauce
- 1/2 cup grated Parmesan cheese
- Fresh basil (optional)

Instructions:

1. Cook the tortellini according to the package instructions. Drain.
2. While the pasta cooks, heat the marinara or Alfredo sauce in a saucepan over medium heat.
3. Toss the cooked tortellini in the sauce, then top with grated Parmesan cheese.
4. Garnish with fresh basil and serve.

Cheeseburger

Ingredients:

- 1 lb ground beef (or turkey)
- 4 hamburger buns
- 4 slices cheddar cheese
- Lettuce, tomato, onion, pickles (optional)
- Ketchup, mustard, mayonnaise (optional)
- Salt and pepper to taste

Instructions:

1. Preheat a grill or skillet over medium-high heat.
2. Form the ground beef into 4 equal patties and season with salt and pepper.
3. Grill the patties for 4-5 minutes per side, or until the desired doneness.
4. Place a slice of cheddar cheese on each patty during the last minute of cooking.
5. Toast the hamburger buns on the grill or in a toaster.
6. Assemble the burgers with your preferred toppings and condiments.
7. Serve immediately.

Pizza Margherita

Ingredients:

- 1 pizza dough (store-bought or homemade)
- 1/2 cup pizza sauce
- 8 oz fresh mozzarella cheese, sliced
- Fresh basil leaves
- 1 tablespoon olive oil
- Salt and pepper to taste

Instructions:

1. Preheat the oven to 475°F (245°C).
2. Roll out the pizza dough onto a baking sheet or pizza stone.
3. Spread a thin layer of pizza sauce over the dough.
4. Arrange the mozzarella cheese slices evenly over the sauce.
5. Bake for 10-12 minutes, until the crust is golden and the cheese is bubbly.
6. Remove from the oven and top with fresh basil leaves.
7. Drizzle with olive oil and season with salt and pepper.
8. Slice and serve warm.

Raclette with Potatoes and Charcuterie

Ingredients:

- 1 lb small baby potatoes, boiled and halved
- 8 oz Raclette cheese, sliced
- Assorted charcuterie (e.g., prosciutto, salami, ham)
- Pickles (e.g., gherkins)
- Fresh herbs (e.g., parsley or thyme)

Instructions:

1. Boil the baby potatoes until tender, then halve them.
2. Arrange the potatoes, charcuterie, and pickles on a platter.
3. Melt the Raclette cheese (using a raclette grill or oven broiler).
4. Pour the melted cheese over the potatoes and charcuterie.
5. Garnish with fresh herbs and serve immediately.

Cottage Cheese Pancakes

Ingredients:

- 1 cup cottage cheese
- 1/2 cup flour
- 2 eggs
- 1 tablespoon sugar
- 1 teaspoon vanilla extract
- 1/4 teaspoon salt
- 1 tablespoon butter (for frying)

Instructions:

1. In a bowl, whisk together the cottage cheese, flour, eggs, sugar, vanilla, and salt until smooth.
2. Heat a skillet over medium heat and add a small amount of butter.
3. Pour spoonfuls of the batter into the skillet and cook for 2-3 minutes on each side, until golden brown.
4. Serve with maple syrup, fresh fruit, or a dusting of powdered sugar.

Cheese Nachos

Ingredients:

- 1 bag tortilla chips
- 2 cups shredded cheddar cheese
- 1 cup shredded Monterey Jack cheese
- 1/2 cup sliced jalapeños (optional)
- Sour cream and salsa for serving

Instructions:

1. Preheat the oven to 350°F (175°C).
2. Arrange the tortilla chips in a single layer on a baking sheet.
3. Sprinkle the shredded cheeses evenly over the chips.
4. Add sliced jalapeños on top if desired.
5. Bake for 10-12 minutes, or until the cheese is melted and bubbly.
6. Serve with sour cream and salsa.

Cheese Puffs

Ingredients:

- 1/2 cup all-purpose flour
- 1/2 teaspoon baking powder
- 1/4 teaspoon salt
- 1/2 cup grated Parmesan cheese
- 1/2 cup shredded cheddar cheese
- 2 eggs
- 1/4 cup milk
- 2 tablespoons butter, melted

Instructions:

1. Preheat the oven to 375°F (190°C) and grease a mini muffin tin.
2. In a bowl, mix together the flour, baking powder, salt, Parmesan, and cheddar cheese.
3. In a separate bowl, whisk together the eggs, milk, and melted butter.
4. Combine the wet and dry ingredients and mix until smooth.
5. Spoon the batter into the muffin tin, filling each cup about halfway.
6. Bake for 10-12 minutes, until golden brown.
7. Serve warm.

Mac and Cheese Pizza

Ingredients:

- 1 pizza dough (store-bought or homemade)
- 1/2 cup pizza sauce
- 2 cups cooked macaroni
- 1 cup shredded cheddar cheese
- 1/2 cup mozzarella cheese
- 1/4 cup breadcrumbs
- Fresh parsley for garnish

Instructions:

1. Preheat the oven to 475°F (245°C).
2. Roll out the pizza dough and place it on a baking sheet or pizza stone.
3. Spread a thin layer of pizza sauce on the dough.
4. Top with cooked macaroni, cheddar cheese, and mozzarella.
5. Sprinkle breadcrumbs on top for crunch.
6. Bake for 10-12 minutes, or until the crust is golden and the cheese is melted.
7. Garnish with fresh parsley and serve.

Baked Cheese-Stuffed Peppers

Ingredients:

- 4 bell peppers, tops cut off and seeds removed
- 1 cup cooked rice
- 1 cup shredded mozzarella cheese
- 1/2 cup grated Parmesan cheese
- 1/4 cup chopped fresh basil
- 1/4 teaspoon garlic powder
- Salt and pepper to taste

Instructions:

1. Preheat the oven to 375°F (190°C).
2. Mix the cooked rice, mozzarella, Parmesan, basil, garlic powder, salt, and pepper in a bowl.
3. Stuff the bell peppers with the cheese and rice mixture.
4. Place the stuffed peppers in a baking dish and cover with foil.
5. Bake for 25-30 minutes, then uncover and bake for an additional 10 minutes to brown the cheese.
6. Serve warm.

Cheese Focaccia

Ingredients:

- 2 1/2 cups all-purpose flour
- 1 teaspoon salt
- 1 tablespoon sugar
- 1 packet active dry yeast
- 1 cup warm water
- 1/4 cup olive oil
- 1 cup shredded mozzarella cheese
- Fresh rosemary for garnish

Instructions:

1. In a bowl, mix the flour, salt, sugar, and yeast. Add warm water and mix to form a dough.
2. Knead the dough for 5-7 minutes, then place in an oiled bowl and cover. Let rise for 1 hour.
3. Preheat the oven to 375°F (190°C).
4. Punch down the dough and shape it into a rectangular shape on a baking sheet.
5. Drizzle olive oil over the dough, then sprinkle with mozzarella cheese and fresh rosemary.
6. Bake for 15-20 minutes, until golden brown.
7. Serve warm.

Cheese and Herb Crackers

Ingredients:

- 1 1/2 cups all-purpose flour
- 1 cup grated sharp cheddar cheese
- 2 tablespoons fresh thyme, chopped
- 1/4 teaspoon garlic powder
- 1/4 teaspoon salt
- 1/4 cup cold butter, cubed
- 1/4 cup water

Instructions:

1. Preheat the oven to 350°F (175°C).
2. In a food processor, combine the flour, cheddar cheese, thyme, garlic powder, and salt.
3. Add the cold butter and pulse until the mixture resembles coarse crumbs.
4. Add water and pulse until a dough forms.
5. Roll out the dough on a lightly floured surface to 1/8-inch thickness.
6. Cut the dough into small squares or shapes and place on a baking sheet.
7. Bake for 12-15 minutes, until golden brown.
8. Serve as a snack or with cheese.

Fondue-Stuffed Chicken

Ingredients:

- 4 boneless, skinless chicken breasts
- 1 cup Swiss cheese, shredded
- 1/2 cup Gruyère cheese, shredded
- 1/4 cup dry white wine
- 1/4 teaspoon garlic powder
- Salt and pepper to taste
- 2 tablespoons butter

Instructions:

1. Preheat the oven to 375°F (190°C).
2. In a bowl, mix the Swiss cheese, Gruyère, white wine, garlic powder, salt, and pepper.
3. Slice a pocket into the chicken breasts and stuff with the cheese mixture.
4. Heat butter in a skillet over medium heat and sear the chicken breasts for 2-3 minutes on each side.
5. Transfer the chicken to the oven and bake for 20-25 minutes, until the chicken is cooked through.
6. Serve warm.

Cheese-Stuffed Meatballs

Ingredients:

- 1 lb ground beef
- 1/2 cup breadcrumbs
- 1/4 cup grated Parmesan cheese
- 1 egg
- 1 teaspoon garlic powder
- 1 teaspoon dried oregano
- Salt and pepper to taste
- 1/2 cup mozzarella cheese, cut into small cubes
- 1/2 cup marinara sauce

Instructions:

1. Preheat the oven to 375°F (190°C).
2. In a bowl, combine the ground beef, breadcrumbs, Parmesan cheese, egg, garlic powder, oregano, salt, and pepper.
3. Form the mixture into meatballs, placing a cube of mozzarella in the center of each one.
4. Place the meatballs on a baking sheet and bake for 15-20 minutes, until cooked through.
5. Heat marinara sauce in a saucepan and pour over the baked meatballs.
6. Serve warm.

Burrata with Roasted Vegetables

Ingredients:

- 1 ball of burrata cheese
- 2 cups assorted vegetables (e.g., bell peppers, zucchini, cherry tomatoes, eggplant), cut into chunks
- 2 tablespoons olive oil
- Salt and pepper to taste
- Fresh basil leaves
- Balsamic glaze for drizzling

Instructions:

1. Preheat the oven to 400°F (200°C).
2. Toss the vegetables with olive oil, salt, and pepper, then spread them in a single layer on a baking sheet.
3. Roast the vegetables for 20-25 minutes, until tender and slightly charred.
4. Plate the roasted vegetables and place the burrata cheese in the center.
5. Drizzle with balsamic glaze and garnish with fresh basil leaves.
6. Serve warm or at room temperature.

Roquefort Salad with Pears

Ingredients:

- 4 cups mixed salad greens (e.g., arugula, spinach, or mesclun)
- 2 ripe pears, sliced
- 1/2 cup Roquefort cheese, crumbled
- 1/4 cup candied pecans
- 1/4 cup balsamic vinaigrette

Instructions:

1. In a large bowl, toss the salad greens with the balsamic vinaigrette.
2. Arrange the pear slices on top of the salad.
3. Sprinkle with crumbled Roquefort cheese and candied pecans.
4. Serve immediately.

Cheese and Spinach Calzone

Ingredients:

- 1 pizza dough (store-bought or homemade)
- 1 cup ricotta cheese
- 1/2 cup mozzarella cheese, shredded
- 1/2 cup Parmesan cheese, grated
- 1 cup spinach, cooked and drained
- 1/4 teaspoon garlic powder
- Salt and pepper to taste
- 1 egg (for egg wash)

Instructions:

1. Preheat the oven to 375°F (190°C).
2. Roll out the pizza dough into a circle on a floured surface.
3. In a bowl, mix the ricotta, mozzarella, Parmesan, spinach, garlic powder, salt, and pepper.
4. Spoon the cheese and spinach mixture onto half of the dough circle.
5. Fold the dough over to create a pocket and seal the edges.
6. Brush the top with beaten egg for a golden finish.
7. Bake for 20-25 minutes, until golden brown.
8. Serve warm.

Halloumi Fries

Ingredients:

- 8 oz halloumi cheese, cut into fries or sticks
- 1 tablespoon olive oil
- 1/4 teaspoon paprika
- Salt and pepper to taste
- Lemon wedges for serving

Instructions:

1. Heat olive oil in a skillet over medium heat.
2. Toss the halloumi fries in paprika, salt, and pepper.
3. Fry the halloumi fries in batches for 2-3 minutes per side, until golden brown.
4. Drain on paper towels and serve with lemon wedges.

Sweet and Savory Cheese Strudels

Ingredients:

- 1 sheet puff pastry (store-bought)
- 1/2 cup cream cheese, softened
- 1/2 cup shredded cheddar cheese
- 1/4 cup honey
- 1 tablespoon fresh thyme leaves
- Salt and pepper to taste
- 1 egg (for egg wash)

Instructions:

1. Preheat the oven to 375°F (190°C).
2. Roll out the puff pastry and cut it into rectangles.
3. Mix the cream cheese, cheddar, honey, thyme, salt, and pepper in a bowl.
4. Spoon the mixture onto the center of each pastry rectangle.
5. Fold the pastry over the filling to create a parcel and seal the edges.
6. Brush with the beaten egg for a golden finish.
7. Bake for 15-20 minutes, until puffed and golden.
8. Serve warm.

Eggplant Parmesan

Ingredients:

- 2 medium eggplants, sliced into 1/2-inch rounds
- 1 cup all-purpose flour
- 2 eggs, beaten
- 1 1/2 cups breadcrumbs
- 1 teaspoon garlic powder
- 1 teaspoon dried oregano
- 2 cups marinara sauce
- 1 1/2 cups shredded mozzarella cheese
- 1/2 cup grated Parmesan cheese
- Olive oil for frying

Instructions:

1. Preheat the oven to 375°F (190°C).
2. In a shallow bowl, mix the flour, garlic powder, oregano, salt, and pepper.
3. Dip the eggplant slices first in the flour mixture, then in the beaten eggs, and finally coat them with breadcrumbs.
4. Heat olive oil in a skillet over medium heat and fry the eggplant slices until golden brown on both sides.
5. Arrange the fried eggplant slices in a baking dish, layering with marinara sauce and mozzarella cheese.
6. Sprinkle Parmesan cheese on top and bake for 20-25 minutes, until the cheese is melted and bubbly.
7. Serve warm.

Ricotta Cheesecake

Ingredients:

- 1 1/2 cups ricotta cheese
- 1 cup cream cheese, softened
- 3/4 cup granulated sugar
- 2 teaspoons vanilla extract
- 3 large eggs
- 1/4 cup all-purpose flour
- 1/4 cup heavy cream
- 1 tablespoon lemon zest
- A pinch of salt
- 1 graham cracker crust (store-bought or homemade)

Instructions:

1. Preheat the oven to 325°F (163°C). Grease a 9-inch springform pan and line the bottom with parchment paper.
2. In a large bowl, beat the ricotta, cream cheese, sugar, and vanilla extract until smooth and creamy.
3. Add the eggs, one at a time, beating well after each addition.
4. Stir in the flour, heavy cream, lemon zest, and a pinch of salt.
5. Pour the mixture into the prepared graham cracker crust and smooth the top.
6. Bake for 45-50 minutes, or until the center is set and the top is slightly golden.
7. Let the cheesecake cool in the pan, then refrigerate for at least 4 hours before serving.

Cheddar Popcorn

Ingredients:

- 1/2 cup popcorn kernels
- 1/4 cup unsalted butter, melted
- 1 1/2 cups sharp cheddar cheese, grated
- 1/2 teaspoon garlic powder
- Salt to taste

Instructions:

1. Pop the popcorn kernels using a popcorn maker, stovetop, or microwave.
2. In a large bowl, drizzle the melted butter over the popcorn.
3. Sprinkle the grated cheddar cheese, garlic powder, and salt over the popcorn.
4. Toss the popcorn to coat it evenly with the cheese and seasonings.
5. Serve immediately for a cheesy snack!

Goat Cheese and Beet Salad

Ingredients:

- 4 medium beets, roasted and peeled
- 4 cups mixed greens (arugula, spinach, or mesclun)
- 4 oz goat cheese, crumbled
- 1/4 cup toasted walnuts
- 1/4 cup balsamic vinegar
- 1 tablespoon olive oil
- Salt and pepper to taste

Instructions:

1. Roast the beets by wrapping them in foil and baking at 400°F (200°C) for 45-60 minutes, until tender. Let them cool, then peel and slice into rounds.
2. In a large bowl, toss the mixed greens with olive oil and balsamic vinegar.
3. Add the beet slices, crumbled goat cheese, and toasted walnuts to the salad.
4. Season with salt and pepper, and serve immediately.

Cheese-Stuffed Puffs

Ingredients:

- 1 sheet puff pastry (store-bought)
- 1 cup shredded mozzarella cheese
- 1/2 cup ricotta cheese
- 1/4 cup Parmesan cheese, grated
- 1 teaspoon dried oregano
- 1 egg (for egg wash)
- Salt and pepper to taste

Instructions:

1. Preheat the oven to 400°F (200°C).
2. Roll out the puff pastry on a floured surface and cut it into squares.
3. In a bowl, mix the mozzarella, ricotta, Parmesan, oregano, salt, and pepper.
4. Spoon a small amount of the cheese mixture onto the center of each puff pastry square.
5. Fold the pastry over to create a pocket and seal the edges with a fork.
6. Brush the tops with the beaten egg for a golden finish.
7. Bake for 12-15 minutes, until puffed and golden.
8. Serve warm.

Grilled Cheese with Pesto

Ingredients:

- 2 slices of your favorite bread (sourdough, whole wheat, etc.)
- 2 tablespoons pesto sauce
- 2 slices of cheddar cheese
- 1 tablespoon butter

Instructions:

1. Spread pesto sauce on one side of each slice of bread.
2. Place a slice of cheddar cheese on top of one slice of bread, pesto side up.
3. Top with the other slice of bread, pesto side down.
4. Heat butter in a skillet over medium heat.
5. Grill the sandwich on both sides for 2-3 minutes, until golden brown and the cheese is melted.
6. Serve warm with a side of tomato soup for a classic combination!

Smoked Gouda Mac and Cheese

Ingredients:

- 8 oz elbow macaroni
- 2 cups milk
- 2 tablespoons unsalted butter
- 2 tablespoons all-purpose flour
- 1 cup shredded smoked Gouda cheese
- 1 cup shredded sharp cheddar cheese
- Salt and pepper to taste
- 1/2 teaspoon garlic powder
- 1/2 cup breadcrumbs (optional, for topping)

Instructions:

1. Cook the macaroni according to package instructions, then drain and set aside.
2. In a saucepan, melt the butter over medium heat. Whisk in the flour and cook for 1-2 minutes.
3. Gradually add the milk, whisking constantly, until the sauce thickens.
4. Stir in the shredded Gouda and cheddar cheeses, and season with salt, pepper, and garlic powder.
5. Combine the cooked macaroni with the cheese sauce, stirring until well coated.
6. For an extra crunchy topping, sprinkle breadcrumbs over the mac and cheese and broil for 2-3 minutes until golden.
7. Serve immediately.